The Good Days

Also by Saradha Koirala

Poetry

Wit of the Staircase (2009)
Tear Water Tea (2013)
Photos of the Sky (2018)

Fiction

Lonesome When You Go (2016)
Learning to Love Blue (2021)

The Good Days

SARADHA KOIRALA

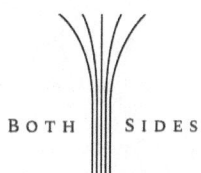

We acknowledge the Traditional Owners of the unceded land on which we write and work: the Wurundjeri Woi Wurrung people of the Kulin nation, and pay our respects to Elders past, present and emerging.

© Saradha Koirala 2025

This book is copyright, apart from any fair dealing as permitted under the Copyright Act and no part may be reproduced without permission from the publisher.

 A catalogue record for this book is available from the National Library of Australia

ISBN: 978-0-6451993-3-8

First published: 2025
Cover Design: Jason Strachan

BOTH SIDES BOOKS

Pascoe Vale South
VIC 3044 Australia
saradhakoirala.com

For Lotus and Finch

Contents

I

Passage	10
The bikes	12
In place	14
That summer I was reading *A brief history of seven killings*	16
Reading Medea on the train	17
Situational awareness	18
I still call writing days writing days	19
Tātou tātou e	20
Borders	21
Ubud	23
New Year	24

II

Trying	28
Morphology	29
March 2020	30
Waking life	31
Learning to be gentle	32
The numbers	33
Anxiety poem	34
The first	36
Good days	37

III
Glue	40
Waste not	42
A whole journey of stars	43
Your baby	44
Anything you can do I can do in a tutu	46
The bikes revisited	47
Resolve	48

IV
I have essays to mark	52
Kite-heart	53
She said *Write these are the good days on the bathroom mirror* but I didn't	55
Vinyasa	56

Notes and Acknowledgements   58

I

Passage

Auckland, New Zealand 1942
The man who will become my Grandad waits by the gangway of the Devonport ferry. Yesterday, he missed his usual trip home and took the later ride. He's decided now to always be late, deliberately miss the more convenient passage home and wait half an hour for the one 'the most beautiful woman he's ever seen' will be on. He steps into the queue just in time to walk on board with her. Later, at a dance, she throws confetti on him like a prophecy. The woman becomes my Grandma, of course.

Pokhara, Nepal 1978
The other man who becomes my Grandad quietly follows his son to the bus stop, where a significant goodbye takes place. His son stays on board with the woman he loves for as long as he can then watches the bus leave. As it happens, they meet again, become my parents, but now he needs the comforting arm his father predicted. Both men walk home together, tears along the dusty road.

Melbourne, Australia 2017

I'm on a train, swiping left, left, left. Attraction exists not in digital form, a few bad snaps of your weekend shenanigans and a poorly written bio. I look up to see people interacting with the space around them, the way they hold themselves as they stand, their expressions, absorbed in their own distractions – paperbacks and podcasts, a phone conversation. Someone photographs the sunrise. I hear a favourite song tinnily through someone else's headphones. I'm trying to get to work.

The bikes

In the 80s bikes were
handed
down from someone taller
gearless
back pedal braking
daydreamer

I rode so slowly I
ended up on the ground

daily lessons in
momentum and

the way a knee-scab dries, lifts
from the outside edges in.

90s bikes faux mountain bikes
Shimano gears a point of pride

fluorescent touches on the frame

double tow-bar   car rack   family weekends

there have always been bikes.

The red one that moved

house to house with each break up

makeshift shelter beneath outside stairs
or leaning against a laundry wall

still so much to learn

about hills and hearts
about maintenance
about holding on.

Red was my favourite   /   my next bike was blue

bought days
after I changed my life
for a love that matched in hue

I fell off into a rosemary bush
smelt amazing, sure

but it let me down
again and again
flat tyres
slackened chain

forever loosening the brakes
so a buckled wheel   can still turn.

In place

I'm digging beneath trellised nasturtium in the garden
       of someone new
planting star jasmine in the sun as
a rain cloud approaches
       but it's the other kind I long to breathe in
the kind of jasmine that gushes over fences, escapes
rambling front gardens, permeates shared paths. I pick
sprigs of it always, carry it
       until it wilts, it carries me.

So much has happened and I wanted to tell you
astounded at my capacity to forgive
I've opened my heart to the gently damaged people of
this world over and over, let them project
       their hurt onto me.
       I get it, but I won't do that anymore.
They seek help or not, move back home as I work
through, work through, work through
soil under my fingernails the smell of almost-rain.

I've decided to tell the truth now. Stop listening to that
voice in my head that nags at me to speak aloud the
words   and just speak aloud

      the damn words.
I've lived long hours in transit, just to reconnect.

It seems everything I've ever written has been a
metaphor for clouds:

looking down on them from planes, watching them roll
in darkly from the east, trusting they'll rain themselves
empty or just move on.
      It's always been about clouds.

The way they look reflected on the water's surface, dis-
tracting me from   the reedy depths.

Seasons change and I let anniversaries pass through me
like a southerly at first,
but even the wind feels warmer when you turn
     your cheek to it.
The red flag of that first betrayal wilts like picked jas-
mine fades in the briefly sunlit garden of someone new.

That summer I was reading *A brief history of seven killings*

a weighty hardback issued from the library. Too heavy to lug out to parks or café courtyards, it anchored me into my new home. I lounged on the daybed and when people asked aloud what I'd been doing, the book's title drew out my kiwi accent almost as thick as the tome itself. A reminder of the recency of my migration.

An odd choice of book, perhaps, but anchored by it I watched the sun pass through the house and when I needed a break from the intensity, I walked to the supermarket in my new neighbourhood; each day a little taller, feeling more present. Roses bent their heads over picket fences and I learnt to recognise those worth stopping to breathe with. I took in the street names, smiled at locals, became one.

Reading Medea on the Train

I stand for the woman whose feet
strain at the straps of her shoes
stare daggers at the snorer
slumped in priority seats.

The 7am chorus tells
of a recent Greek wedding
her brother's I think
the audience invested as recorded festivities
fill the carriage from a phone.

Jason's woken early, texts
a busy day ahead
while his paged namesake remains
oblivious to how his day will unfold.

At work we'll be promised an ending
as long as we plan the next beginning
Medea's children smile at her
and she breaks down again.

I give her one more station
to change her mind.

Situational Awareness
for all those who never made it home

What were you doing alone in a park at night?
with your violent thoughts morphing into violent acts
the way fear twists as streetlights disappear behind you.

What were you thinking dressed like that in the dark?
grey hoodie hiding your face disguising
your dangerous form as a shapeless blur of nothing.

Were you never taught to stay in the light where we can
see you? or to call a friend if you felt that surging desire
to hurt someone, take what you had no right to touch?

When murderous thoughts cast tree-like shadows across
your mind did you not know to clench your fist
around your car keys as a reminder of your strength

reminder you're a threat? Keep your distance.
This park is no place for you lit candles erase darkness
and the silence is on our side now.

From this muddy soccer field sprouts a shrine of flowers
laid by everyone who's ever said
be safe, let me know when you've made it home.

I still call writing days writing days

but really they've become
sleeping late under a pile of cats days
letting my washed hair dry in the sun days
lunchtime yoga class followed by lunch days
reading poetry in a café, scribbling notes
in my journal days

slow stride along the bike path back to the space
where maidenhair ferns its way down one wall
devil's ivy curls its lips like leaves to the light
thick arms of monstera fill the corner window
obscuring a laundry line of last week's life

heartbeat rhythm of solitude, solace, self-solicitude days.

Tātou tātou e
After the Christchurch mosque shootings

A song from my childhood fills the room

students stand   watch   me

awkward

when my country is mentioned

they think of their teacher   turn

        seek

my expression   in assembly hall crowd

because I'm usually smiling

when I'm reminded of home.

Borders

Sometimes I'm that puzzle you bought from an op-shop
five dollars. You looked so pleased holding it
under your arm a rubber band snapped tight
around the cardboard box, seasonally appropriate image
of red and yellow leaves above a thick black river.

When we spread it on the kitchen table and sifted
pieces through fingers, fingers through pieces
we couldn't find a single edge to get us started
– not a single edge or corner – five bucks, sure
but it was hard not to feel let down.

There are times on the train when young men sit near
and speak softly to each other in the familiar cadence
of my father's language. I want to tell them I know
I'm related to them, just look at my name
but it's a language I only recognise by sound.

Or when I hand over my keep cup and the vowels
of the barista are clipped like mine, hanging pounamu
and I want to say bro, we're bonded, secret handshake
but there are hundreds of us here
with nothing remarkable about our easy migration.

Anyway, it turns out you can still put a puzzle together
when the edges are missing, but it's harder to trust
the process, harder to immerse yourself in the task
when you don't really know if the bit you're looking for
is lost in someone else's living room miles from here.

The trick is to start from the middle.
Work your way from the bright centre
of autumnal leaves towards forested outskirts
like an ever-expanding universe
trying not to think what will happen

when eventually
inevitably
there will be no
spare pieces left.

Ubud

A hummingbird hovers through bougainvillea
we watch from the pool's edge
30 degrees until it's not
straight lines of downpour brighten

greens and crimsons
red birds of paradise
frangipani yellow and pink
clustered on leafless branches.

The river rises then
villas across the valley obscured in mist
fat drops fall until the clouds are empty
drip musically from thatched edges.

Logs of bamboo gather at the river's sharpest bend
and the sun's revealed just in time
to set a blood stain behind palm tops
gold through the upstairs window.

New Year

I didn't realise the front yard was so large until you
took to it in gardening gloves, trimmed back the privet.
Cleared spaces filled with possibilities and native grasses.

As last year changed from this year, and
I could stop saying 'last year' with such portent, such
regret; a phrase loaded with the weight of an on-coming
sob-story, we were camping by the Wellington river.

A settlement of pegged-out shelters,
fairy lights and bonfires
I was miles from my Wellington home.

I say the h word again with a kind of inflection
trying it out for size

sighing out the *həʊ*, the *m* buzzes past my lips
I hold it in my mouth like a pill.

This constant starting over exhausts me. Always has.
Newness of a cleared front yard.
I'll dig in my toes, resolve

to thicken like the trunk of a grapevine, let the porch
be built around me for a change.

Disturbing the privet is making my eyes stream
but on New Year's Day
I sprained my finger, slipped on rocks in
flimsy jandals, a little drunk.

There were bull ant bites on the tops of my feet and a
blush of sunburn between my breasts.

What I mean is, these things pass, they clear up.
We heal and adapt.
We look back and see fairy lights strung between trees
flickering with comforting regularity, we move closer to
each other on an old brown couch.

We look back and then we don't look back.

II

Trying

I take a blood test like an exam
high cholesterol, low vitamin D
the numbers bold and red on the print-out.

Sun's been lazy recently
so I hunt down supplements
little drops of captured light.

Yesterday in bed my thin brown forearm
came into focus
resting across both bodies.

A crease at the crook of my elbow
familiar freckles a pebbled path
towards my ageing wrist,

hand, fingers, nails that need cutting.
This has always been my arm, I thought,
this has been me all along.

Morphology

We saw you on the fourth day of spring.
Still part of me and in ghostly black and white
but there you were, like a photo of the moon.

The sonographer chatted the whole way through
recommending nappy brands and hypnobirthing.
We could see your bones, your organs and eyeballs.

You are beautiful and perfect and even if you weren't
you still would be. When we stepped outside
jasmine was everywhere, new blossom

on the otherwise bare twigs of winter. The next time
we see you you'll be entering the world, exiting the world
you've made your own and joining

this marvellous place of birdsong and magnolia.
Each day the temperature rises gently, our body swells
ripples of your quickening strengthen

your underwater dance
beating heart, undeniable presence of being.

March 2020

The world is told to self-isolate just
as I might feel like mingling with the world again
I get Friday mornings off to shower, cut my nails
drink tea while it's still hot. Rainbows in the living room
I walk around the block

collect two fallen frangipani flowers
an autumn garden inconsistency. Summer
a blur of pregnancy birth baby
two months measured out in feeds and naps
tears, each week I walk this walk a little quicker

each week things get better before they get hard again
but mostly there are more good days than tricky days
and never do I call them bad days.
One of my flowers blows to the ground

face-plants grass, stem to the sky
the other I hold as I write, bringing it to my nose
with each pause of the pen, sun-warmed black-clad body
Kmart shapewear holds my weakened core together

I swing my briefly baby-free arms about
the scent of good days and tricky days ahead.

Waking life

Each night in the new house I farewell former lives
through broken sleep dreams.

Spot a high school crush, now mid-forties
soft about the jaw, the soft hue of his roots.

Old partners with mail they'd neglected to redirect
challenge me to a game in the penny arcade.

Night after night the past appears
asking if I'm sure, and I'm sure

I wake to my baby again and again
fall asleep to reply

I choose the life I wake to
I wake to this life and I choose it
again and again and again.

Learning to be gentle

I keep my judgements to myself, mostly
a cat claw stuck in the baby's sleeve
causes more tears

than her top teeth pushing through gums.
Those stubborn numbers
finally in sharp descent

then clusters form from a reckless traveller
and borders are drawn again.
We visit every playground we can

turn the pram around so she faces
the world head on.
I must be feeling optimistic.

The step into the sunroom becomes
a literal tipping point
when thresholds are ignored

like firm pats on a patient cat's back
until the patience of the cat snaps too.

The numbers

Every morning I check the numbers:
Covid cases and hours of sleep.

Try to focus on the rolling average forest
not the trees, though they blossom and bud.

It's been a year of seasons. I mean, of course it has
but so much so this time. We spent money on

woollen things to wrap around us
and from this end of it all I'm glad

to have hunkered down through the worst of it.
Hair growing unruly and the same two outfits.

I buy sparkly skirts in preparation
for whatever good things are surely about to happen

and on the morning after she first sleeps
straight through twelve of the night's twelve hours

I walk to the corner store for bread and eggs
feeling extraordinarily ordinary again.

Anxiety poem

We count out the things taken from us
handed back nestled in conditions
permissions and we're so grateful
so grateful for the simple gift
of driving to the supermarket

sitting up in the trolley like an adventure
choosing snacks for our drive back home
we're so grateful, so lucky
to be able to drive to the supermarket together.

We walk around the block, hoping to bump
into someone never dobbing in the neighbours
we're happy to see them
happy to stand in the street and talk to
their aunty, their mother, their entire family

the pavement becomes our meeting place
kids sharing toys, drawing worms and flowers
drawing hearts and rhinos and we're so lucky
so grateful for the company, so lucky to have each other.

Our radius expands and we could go to the city
but our circle is set, not ready to be stretched and besides
we're so lucky, so grateful. It's a numbers game as always
one shot, two shots, dates and percentages
kilometres from home, hours of exercise

how many friends can you fit on a picnic rug?
how many friends do you still have and we'll get there
we say, we're counting on it, counting and counting
conversations edited to how are you getting on
we'll get there. We're lucky, we're counting, we're lucky.

Any other year of my life, I say, any other year and this
would be unbearable. We can't know what it's like
for everyone else, but we know we're lucky, grateful
counting our lucky stars, counting our blessings
counting and counting and counting.

The first

Our world shrunk down to the three of us
just as it had expanded to the three of us.

So safe that when you fell, pushing
your plastic trolley around the block blood

shocked to panic and the first ever band aid
you held your hand in a protective fist

grazed thumb resting on top
doing everything one-handed for days.

We did our bit, did our best did
what we were told week after weakening

week we rose from bed every
                                              single
morning
                  to you   to the world

      to the hardening
                       scab

of a tiny thumb's first   bright wound.

Good days

On a good day I'll remember my mask
after I've shut the door

go back inside for it and realise
the sun pushes lace and leaf

shadows around my daughter's room
all morning

toys spread with careful
abandon mid-play

on a good day
I've spent an hour or two forgetting

I'll need a mask
if we go out there.

III

Glue

I've glued my daughter's hair clips back together
pink fabric ripped, but salvageable and with
a small blue heart from my own broken earrings.

I could ride my bike to the mall right now
buy them ten times over, buy the brightest ones
the most expensive ones, ones that will survive

small fingers and curiosity. They've lasted less
than two months, the trip to Kmart her first time using
a public toilet, everything an adventure

after months of lockdown, everything an adventure
when you're not-quite two. I could buy her new hair clips
every day, but I won't because one bedtime meltdown

she'd been moved away from the cat, who
puts up with more than he should, though loved
puts up with so much she thinks his tail is fair game.

She's still learning not to squeeze so hard. I took her
to her room, wiped streaks of tears sat opposite,
a pale green swaddle from newborn days draped

over her head and mine as she calmed, held
my face with the gentleness I know she has gentleness
I hope for her, but hope will not be her undoing

as it so often has felt like mine…

Thank you for my joy, Mummy I checked I'd understood,
Your joy? Yes. Thank you for my joy.
Thank you for dinner, Mummy. hands still gentle,

the same hands that dissected hair clips
beat fists on the ground, made the cat flinch
Thank you for my sparkly hair clips from Kmart, Mummy.

So I've glued them back together, adding a piece
of me, knowing we'll break and renew each other
twenty more times before morning.

Waste not

If I were my mother I would cut the bitten
and brown bits from my daughter's
collection of abandoned apples
cook them in a small pot
eat them with muesli and yoghurt.

If I were my Grandmother I would never
have given a whole apple
to a child in the first place, but slivered it
into sharable pieces
arranged neatly on a plate for all.

I try to be a good mother
never raising my voice or hand
but I've always been awkward about fruit
buying blueberries out of season
just because I can.

I try to protect my daughter from the
browning and bitten parts of the world
but can only think guiltily
of the apple crumble recipe
I looked up but won't be using.

A whole journey of stars

At two and a half she's big enough
to do most things by herself, proudly declares
I don't need anyone, as she climbs
the once Himalayan steps
to the top of the slide.

At two and a half she's still excited
to unbox the same toy over and over
a stack of glow in the dark plastic
amazing every time and no less so to me
when she wows at *a whole journey of stars!*

At two and a half, she's still small enough
to fall asleep in my arms
if fever hits, or a long haul flight
even then she will defy me
no, no, no, softly from furrowed dreams.

Your baby

At our eight week scan we said *we're just checking
if there's a baby growing in Mummy's tummy
I don't think there will be* you said but this time I was sure.

The sonographer said *how cute, so cute*
this morphing little mass with a beating heart
grainy wiggly thing we could barely make out.

From then on you were obsessed with babies, stuffing
small teddies down your top *shush shush shushing* them as
if you remembered being *shush shush shushed* yourself.

Who showed you how to hold a baby? I asked as you cradled
the head of a stiff plastic doll gazed lovingly
into its unblinking eyes *You did when you held me* you said.

As my belly grew you said yours did too would repeat
with your own pronouns *I can feel her moving, she's making
me tired* and we recognised the empathy with interest.

You found a pink onesie for your baby at Savers
and a small dress that matched your party dress
kept aside a blanket covered in hearts.

Then our baby came in a rush and a gush teeth-in-the-
pillow pain but over so fast my body shook in shock and
joy his hot little slippery-fish body in my arms.

You loved him straight away, spoke softly let him
curl his tiny fingers around yours. You said you were still
waiting for your baby, you were starting to get impatient.

When I asked if it was real or pretend you said *Real of
course* and I said *Oh* she was going to come on your third
birthday you said so we sat you down told you *grown-ups
have babies, not big kids* we were sorry and you argued sadly

then hardly spoke again about your baby. But when you
did we said, *Remember grown ups have babies*
and you assured us *my baby's coming soon
so we won't have to talk about it anymore.*

Our baby was weighed and measured growing healthy
and strong at eight weeks old I heard your dad remind
you *Mummy's tummy grew so big, she was tired, we had to go
to the hospital in the middle of the night. Babies are a lot of work.*

Nine months after that eight week scan you took
the pink onesie from your drawer and the dress
that matched your party dress, you took the blanket
covered in hearts and offered them to your baby brother

never mentioning your own baby again.

Anything you can do I can do in a tutu

On her third birthday my daughter
bites her friend for saying there is a wolf
in Goldilocks and the Three Bears
and I know she got this from me
not the biting, perhaps the temper but certainly
a dedication to stories and truth.

More bear than Goldilocks herself these days
six weeks of being a big sister — a role she takes to heart
means six weeks of no longer being narrator.
She climbs to the top of the volcano at Funtopia
in tutu and sparkly shoes
carries a stick with her wherever she goes.

The bikes revisited

When the smallest
one sleeps
released gently from
arms to bed
I roll my shoulders drag
the exercise bike
out from its dusty corner point
it towards the glass
backdoor climb on and ride.

A stationary journey out
doors and over
deck above laundry
line and ornamental pear
tree I fly like the kids at
the end of E.T
high above the neighbour's
shed until his cry
brings me back to land.

Resolve

From the too early to ask but wanting to know
to the shared wanting the trying the monthly redstain no.

From the blood tests and food shifts
to the caffeine withdrawal and supplements

from the trying some more to the relief and amazement
to the dance in the living room joy.

From the tired to the queasy to the secret until
safe to tell for the congratulations.

From the swelling to the scans the nervous to the healthy
other parents' stories from the horror to the perfect.

From the haemorrhoids that passed to the ones that bled
through maternity dress on the morning train.

From the slow slow walk to the tired tired tired
from the phone scroll waiting to the waters breaking.

From the induction to the horse breath waves
of squeeze and release to the remember the horse breath

the pushing and crying the holding and feeding
from the crying and the crying and crying.

From the leaking to the feeding the pooping the leaking
the waking and waking to the crying some more.

From the pain to the fever hot red rocks of infection
to the antibiotics to the happening again.

From the lockdowns the masks to the walks the curfews
the radius to the zooming and slowing down.

From the packing and moving to the solving and solving
from the crawling to the sickness the steps the words.

From the washing to the laundry the soaking and drying
to the nappies the laundry the food on the floor.

From the potty to the wetting the frustration the refusing
from the anxiety to the getting it but anxiety still there.

From the wanting only mummy to never wanting mummy from the going back to work and never having time.

From the wanting again to the saying it out loud
from the positive test to the covid positive test.

From the scans to the appointments, the explaining
the announcement to the excitement

the exhaustion at the thought
of the crying the waking the leaking ahead.

From the nausea to the magnesium to the virus again
to the tired the tired the tired…

From the meltdowns to the accidents the shouting and
biting too tired too big now to hide build forts carry run.

From the wait wait wait to the sudden gut punch
and gush from the rush to the shout to the boy.

From the coming home to the blurry
to the cuddles and recovery.

From the sweetness to the adjustment the struggling
to adjust from the meltdowns to the sleep, oh the sleep.

From the feeding to the social not wanting to miss out
from the things being open please keep being open.

From the trips to the flights the long long haul
from the family to the home again to the growing.

From the jet lag to the waking winter setting in
from the sleep coming back the good sleeper is back.

From the real estate agents to the doctors
to being blindsided by news

from this thing to the next thing and the next, carry on.

IV

I have essays to mark

and my toddler sleeps on me all afternoon
his breathing heavy through snot
he won't let me clean from his nose.

I have essays to mark and I marked some earlier
when he napped and it wasn't yet clear
that he was coming down with yet another bug
that makes him warm and sleepy and snotty.

I have essays to mark and I promise my students
they'll get them back before their exam on Tuesday
a promise I'll have to keep because after Tuesday
I'll have exams to mark.

I have essays to mark, essays that were written
while I supervised at my laptop writing reports
on the morning my son was at daycare
catching a new virus just in time for the weekend.

I have essays to mark and I need a snack
but my small warm boy rests heavily, breathes heavily
on me so I close my eyes to the darkening room
let my body rise and fall with his.

Kite-heart

Onesies and tulle dresses billowed out then defied their own pegs. Tiny socks spread themselves about the garden, but at least it all dried. And a good laundry day is a good kite flying day.

We stuffed the nine-dollar kite into a pannier, rainbow tail flapping eagerly, and rode down to the reserve to set it free, let it tug us gently, let it let us tug it gently back.

The kids got bored long before I did, ran to the playground with Jason, so I took the reins, allowing the kite to swoop and loop, watching it try to arc gracefully through the ground and falling short.

Each crash my cue to wind the string up, haul it back in, but before I could pack it down completely the wind would grab it again and off it went, off I went letting out its lead with a click click click of the wrist. Our dance of pull and release. Every time: a crash, a gather, a gust, and a yield.

At one point the wind blew hair across my face and when I cleared my view I thought the kite was a heart.

Not the squashy bulging forms my daughter has learnt to draw on birthday cards, but a proper anatomically correct blood pumping organ. My own old blood pumper flying as free as one can when they're tethered to the ground by the constant call of Mummy Mummy Mummy.

Or was it my own child pulling the cord to come, come but asking me to stay? Let out more string, it seemed to say, long enough to let me dance in the high air you'll never reach but don't let me go.

Either way the kite remained at the mercy of my flicking wrist and the wind itself, until it was us — my kite-heart-child and I — co-conspirators putting the wind to task, daring it, forcing it to keep us aloft.

She said *write these are the good days on the bathroom mirror* but I didn't

not because I'm tired
constantly aware of the soft weight of my limbs
as they call to be raised
placed into position
as if duty is a dance instructor
correcting my pose

but because the first deep breath each morning
as I take the steps two at a time
to hoist up the blind, reveal
a still pale sky
cityscape and balloons rising, igniting

allows me to hear the rustle
of my waking children
who will smell of night breath and being small.

Vinyasa

Once a week the door clicks closed at 6.15am
it's 9 degrees, it's 5 degrees
the car interior warms at my demand
tea in a takeaway mug.

The first time I brought my own mat so long had it been
that I'd forgotten the corner of stacked rolls, foam
blocks, floral bolsters, cupboard of clean white blankets.

Not so long though that my body couldn't yield and turn
hands reach for the ceiling, towards the back
of the room planted neatly next to foot.

I want to inhale the scent of being alive.
So cold here now that nothing seems to warm
enough to let off even a slight smell
not even the gum trees ground me anymore.

The room lightens as the day begins
rubbish truck clanking down Sydney road
the traffic a steady chant of om…

the practice ends. I drive through lit city mindful
of lane changes, hook turns, thick soy chai latte
poetry podcast, earrings and work shoes on.

Notes and Acknowledgements

Many of these poems have appeared in draft form on my website www.saradhakoirala.com and as Instagram reels. Thank you to all who have followed, reacted, commented and encouraged me.

'March 2020' was read on Radio NZ as the world was going into pandemic lockdown: March 2020. Thank you to Jesse Mulligan and the producers of his show for supporting my poetry at this time.

'Tātou tātou e' refers to the mass shootings that occurred at Al Noor Mosque and Linwood Islamic Centre in Christchurch on 15th March 2019.

'Situational awareness' is a response to the rape and murder of Euradyce Dixon in a Melbourne park on 13th June 2018.

I am grateful to the judges and administrators of the 2023 Kathleen Grattan Poetry Award, for which a version of this manuscript was shortlisted.

Thank you to Lotus and Finch for transforming me into a parent — you both bring me so much joy and have changed the way I see the world.

And to Jason, who I met two days after the first poem in this book was written: these last eight years have been some seriously good days. This is a book of us — thank you for everything.

www.ingramcontent.com/pod-product-compliance
Lightning Source LLC
Chambersburg PA
CBHW032338300426
44109CB00041B/1291